DIANA

THE LIFE AND LEGACY
OF THE PEOPLE'S PRINCESS

DIANA

THE LIFE AND LEGACY
OF THE PEOPLE'S PRINCESS

BRIAN HOEY

Contents

Prologue

On Sunday 31 August 1997, the nation awoke to the news that Diana, Princess of Wales had died.

As someone who had the privilege of meeting Diana on several occasions, I still find it difficult to believe that this event that shocked the world took place more than a quarter of a century ago. The recollection of that fateful summer day still reverberates, and for many, like me, the memories remain fresh.

Diana, Princess of Wales was just 36 years old when she died in the early hours of that August day in 1997 in a horrific car crash in Paris, along with her friend, Dodi Fayed, the son of Mohamad al-Fayed who was at that time the owner of Harrods, London's most famous department store.

More than 25 years on, within the Royal Family itself there have been many changes: numerous births, several marriages and, naturally, the deaths of some main characters. Queen Elizabeth II's sister, Princess Margaret, died on 9 February 2002 at the age of 71. Just seven weeks later, on 30 March, their mother, the 101-year-old Queen Mother, died at her home, Royal Lodge in Windsor Great Park. On 9 April 2021, Prince Philip, the Duke of Edinburgh, to whom The Queen had been married

for 73 years, died just weeks before his 100th birthday. Most significantly of all, Queen Elizabeth II died at Balmoral on 8 September 2022 at the age of 96.

However, the joyous news of the birth of a child has been celebrated many times in the Royal Family since 1997. The Queen had two more grandchildren: Lady Louise Mountbatten-Windsor and James Mountbatten-Windsor, Viscount Severn, born in 2003 and 2007 respectively, the children of Her Majesty's youngest son, Prince Edward, Earl of Wessex. The Queen also become a great-grandmother many times over, with her first great-grandchild, Savannah Phillips, daughter of Peter Phillips, arriving in 2010.

Of all the royal marriages that have taken place over that period, three are of particular historic note. The first came in 2005, when Prince Charles and Camilla Parker Bowles (who in September 2022 became Her Majesty the Queen Consort) were married in a civil ceremony at Windsor Guildhall; constitutional issues made it inappropriate for them, as divorcees, to be married in church, but a service of prayer and dedication, led by the Archbishop of Canterbury and held in St George's Chapel in the grounds of Windsor Castle, followed the legal ceremony.

In 2011 came the wedding of Diana's eldest son, Prince William, to Catherine Middleton, a vivacious and charming girl from an ordinary middle-class family from the Home Counties. Now the Prince and Princess of Wales, their marriage has been blessed by the births of their three children: George, Charlotte and Louis. In 2018, Diana's younger son, Prince Harry, married Meghan Markle, an American divorcee. His wife had been little known in the United Kingdom previously; she was best known as an actress in the television drama series *Suits*, filmed in Canada for the cable network USA, and their union brought a sprinkle of Hollywood glamour to the Royal Family. On the day they were married, Her Majesty created Harry and Meghan Duke and Duchess of Sussex; they now have two children, Archie and Lilibet. In 2020, in a move that disappointed many people in Britain, not least of all the Royal Family, the couple decided to leave the country of Harry's birth and live in the United States to seek financial independence and what they described as the privacy they were denied in the UK.

There have, of course, also been other less than happy newsworthy events. In 2002, Diana's former butler, Paul Burrell, was accused of stealing 310 items belonging to her, Prince Charles and Prince William. But the sensational trial collapsed dramatically when The Queen remembered that Burrell had told her previously that he had taken the items into his own possession for safe keeping. Closer to home was the scandal surrounding The Queen's second son, Prince Andrew, Duke of York, which in 2022 resulted in him being deprived of his military roles and royal patronages, and unable to carry out public duties, although he escorted Her Majesty into Westminster Abbey for his father's memorial service in March that year.

But members of the Royal Family have a high sense of self-preservation and they are experts in what they describe as 'strategic ambiguity', so they have taken all these ups and downs in their stride. And, unquestionably, these family events, when placed into world context, with its continuing conflicts, unrest, natural disasters and health problems, pale into insignificance.

Remarkably, in the years that have passed since the loss of Diana, Queen Elizabeth II commemorated three Jubilees. Most recent of all was her Platinum Jubilee in 2022 – the same year that she celebrated her 96th birthday – marking her 70 years on the throne. Sadly, it was also the year that Her Majesty died.

All this and much more has happened since Diana died; she now lies at peace in her grave on an island in an ornamental lake at the Althorp family estate in Northamptonshire, which her brother Charles has described as 'an oasis of calm'.

RIGHT: This Doric-style temple at Althorp is a memorial to Diana; at its centre is a black marble silhouette of the princess; either side of this are two stone plaques, one bearing a quote from Diana about her charity work and the other a quote from the eulogy given by her brother, Charles Spencer, at her funeral. The memorial is by the lake surrounding the island that is her final resting place.

The Woman Who Might Have Been Queen

After she married the man who is now our king, Diana was the most famous, photographed and talked about woman in the world. Before that, very few people knew her name and she would have been the first to admit that up to that point she had not achieved anything of particular note.

Everything changed when she began dating Prince Charles; almost overnight, and certainly within a few short months, she was to become the newest star in the most famous family on the planet. When, at the tender age of 19, her engagement to the Prince of Wales was announced, she found herself thrust into the uncompromising formality of life within the House of Windsor.

Diana had that elusive star quality which she managed to combine with the common touch. With her popular 'touchy-feely, hands-on' approach, she positively encouraged people from all walks of life, and from every class, to approach her and to engage with her. Unlike many other royals, she never shied away from physical contact. One of The Queen's ladies-in-waiting explained Diana's tactile approach by saying she was a natural 'hugger and kisser'.

LEFT: With all their hopes and dreams before them, the Prince and Princess of Wales thrilled the crowds when they appeared on the balcony of Buckingham Palace on their wedding day, 29 July 1981.

Diana was always a woman who acted from the heart and the public loved her for it. Her aura of accessibility set her apart from the rest of the Royal Family, so that ordinary members of the public felt they could approach her without any fear of a rebuttal. Diana had the intrinsic ability to communicate with the regular man or woman in the street and for them to identify with her, as she became, in many people's view, the acceptable face of a modern monarchy.

What was it that she possessed that not only made her different from everyone else in the Royal Family, but that also led to her being seen as one of the most attractive woman in history? The answer may be that she exuded a mystique of sheer feminine magnetism that very few other women in history have possessed. That characteristic mesmerised nearly everyone she met and many of those who only viewed her from afar. There were, after all, plenty of women as good-looking as she was, the difference being that she radiated an air of ineffable femininity elusive to many other beautiful women. She also possessed one characteristic that eludes many other members of the Royal Family. Whereas others attract admiration and respect, in varying degrees, Diana was one of those likeable people who made everyone feel they were the most interesting and fascinating person she had ever encountered. Added to this, she also liked to use first names, whoever she was talking to – a simple technique that made them feel ten feet tall.

There were many sides to Diana: the girlish, giggly youngster when she was with her childhood pals; the sex symbol she was sometimes portrayed as by the media; and the sad, vulnerable woman who really wanted nothing more than a happy, loving marriage. Diana did not seek a divorce; she and the Prince of Wales were ordered to go down that route by The Queen following the famous, and unfortunate, television interview Diana gave to the BBC in 1995. The interview was a disaster: Diana memorably said, 'There were three of us in this marriage'; she also cast doubts on Prince Charles ever becoming king, or even wanting to. As far as Diana was concerned, divorce was the last thing she wanted originally; neither did The Queen, but Her Majesty had no option when Diana openly questioned the monarchy. The Queen had to assert her authority as the sovereign and unquestioned head of the House of Windsor: it was a case of sovereignty over family.

Diana could be both confused and confident at the same time, quick-tempered yet instantly forgiving, and, in later life, totally fearless but always passionate. By her own admission, she was not an intellectual and her scholastic record was undistinguished. But she was far from stupid and possessed a native intelligence, as she proved over and over again during her short life by becoming far more than the 'walking clothes horse' some of her detractors claimed her to be.

RIGHT: A formal portrait of the Prince and Princess of Wales in the 1980s; at this time everyone expected Diana would one day be Queen Consort when Charles became sovereign.

Diana was also the woman who compelled other members of the Royal Family to become 'celebrities' in their own right. Whereas before many – with, undoubtedly, some exceptions – had been content to remain aloof, distanced and admired simply because of the accident of their birth, they now had to do something positive in order to attract the public's attention – and gain its affection. Royalty had been seen by some, however unfairly, as mere figureheads, with armies of sycophantic servants prepared to massage their egos, being used to occupying the limelight practically from birth, as if it were their right. For any members of the Royal Family who fell into such categories, Diana's arrival eclipsed them almost overnight and apparently without too much effort on her part; noses were put severely out of joint.

Diana changed any such notions, spreading compassion like honey, hugging sick children and geriatrics with equal enthusiasm. She was photographed nursing a baby suffering from leprosy and holding hands with a young girl maimed by a landmine in Angola. Whereas her sister-in-law, the Princess Royal, who has for years been recognised as one of the hardest-working members of the Royal Family, resolutely refused to comply with the pleas of photographers to pick up small babies in an African village, saying, 'I don't do stunts,' Diana was the complete opposite. She involved herself openly with hundreds of causes, publicly demonstrating her

LEFT: Delighting the crowds, Diana and Charles kiss as she presents him with a prize at a polo match in Windsor Great Park in 1985.

natural instinct to help the underprivileged, the disabled and those suffering disease, ill treatment and malnutrition. And if Diana carried out her work in a vastly different way from much of the rest of the Royal Family, becoming more personally involved and manipulating the media to the advantage of those she sought to help, it worked absolutely brilliantly.

Members of the Royal Family, just like every other kind of 'celebrity' – actors, sporting personalities and politicians – realise the importance of good theatre. Royals know how vital it is to make a favourable impression and possess an innate feeling for doing the right thing in front of the camera and any audience, no matter how large or small: the State Opening of Parliament, royal weddings or just meeting one or two soldiers, preferably heroes, at one of their regiments. From a young age, they begin to understand the difference between being professional and merely amateur, and one thing that is absolutely certain about the royals is that they are all thorough professionals in what they do. Diana became a past master in these arts. She never missed an opportunity to use her wiles in order to gain attention for one of her charitable causes. And she did it to magnificent effect.

The Royal Family has not always taken to outsiders easily, and by that they mean anyone not 'born to the purple' – the 'semi-detached' royals. They may have been forced by circumstances to allow 'commoners' into the family from time to time, as the pool of available – and willing – European royalty dried up, but newcomers were, in the main, admitted on sufferance, and were expected to know their place in the hierarchy. Happily, a more gentle form of royal order has now emerged.

Diana's entry into the Royal Family was difficult almost from day one. She later said she had been given no special training or advice on how to conduct herself. She confirmed that she found the discipline of royal life very hard to become accustomed to in the early days, where every moment was governed by the diary, clock and calendar – as Camilla, now queen consort, also found out years later.

Queen Elizabeth II, a country woman at heart, found it difficult to understand why Diana, always first and foremost a city girl, was unable to settle into life in royal palaces – Her Majesty having herself known nothing else since the age of ten. Equally, Diana found it difficult to see why she should spend hours, days even, in a mausoleum – which is how she once described Buckingham Palace.

The Queen tried to make friends with Diana initially; it was through no deliberate unkindness on her part that they did not get on too well. Her Majesty would invite her new daughter-in-law to join her for luncheon or tea, but both soon discovered that they had little in common. Later, when Diana and Charles were going through their difficult period, Diana went to see Her Majesty several times and on one occasion The Queen's page reported that Diana was crying a lot while she waited to see Her Majesty. The Queen said that Diana cried throughout the visit and wouldn't stop. However, Diana was very fond of the Duke of Edinburgh and, at first, he returned her affection in equal measure. That changed when her public comments, on television and to journalists, threatened the monarchy. After that, there was no longer any strong connection. Prince Philip, just like The Queen, would never allow anything or anyone to damage the institution of monarchy.

Diana may have been viewed as the most glamorous woman in the world but she never put on any airs and graces, and was unafraid to show her emotions in public; her concern for others was palpably genuine. Another of her qualities was her vulnerability; perhaps that is why people sprang to her defence – even when her behaviour later became unpredictable at times. If she seemed to rebel against tradition and protocol, it struck a chord with ordinary people who felt she was striking a blow for them as well. Diana loved the fact that she was loved for what she was.

There was much that set Diana apart from other members of the Royal Family, including a rare combination of star quality and compassion, combined with the graciousness that some of her royal relatives lacked. She also became a fashion icon, her style emulated by millions of women.

But Diana was not perfect. She could be difficult, even manipulative, at times – both with the media, when it suited her, and also the public, many of whom felt she could do no wrong. She was, nevertheless, the woman who changed the way the British Royal Family is viewed today. Without her, it could still be seen as an antiquated institution from centuries past, somewhat out of touch with real life.

Diana was a jewel in the royal crown who could have seen the monarchy safely into the 21st century. This inspirational young woman was to many people, and will always be remembered as, *THE* Princess of Wales.

RIGHT: The Prince and Princess of Wales and their children on a family holiday on the Isles of Scilly in 1989.

LEFT: A family photo of Diana in her pram in the grounds of Park House, Sandringham.

OPPOSITE: An aerial view of Althorp, the family estate of the Earls Spencer. Diana moved here with her father and siblings in 1975.

Royal Connections: The Early Days

The Honourable Diana Frances Spencer was born at Park House on the Sandringham Estate in Norfolk in the late afternoon of 1 July 1961, weighing a respectable 7lbs 12oz (3.5kg). She was christened on 30 August at the Church of St Mary Magdalene (known locally as Sandringham Church) by the Right Reverend Percy Herbert. Her godparents were John Floyd, Alexander Gilmour, Lady Mary Gilmour, Sarah Platt and Carol Fox. On 12 March 1976, when she was 15, Diana was confirmed into the Church of England by the Bishop of Rochester.

The Princess of Wales was not royal by birth, although her family, the Spencers, had been closely associated with royalty since the 17th century when Charles I granted the first Earldom of Sunderland to Henry Spencer who had been wealthy enough to advance the king £10,000 at the outbreak of the Civil War. Even earlier, John Spencer had been knighted by Henry VIII, and another ancestor, Robert Spencer, was made 1st Baron Spencer in 1603.

Robert Spencer became one of the richest men in England and, later, the senior branch of the family became Dukes of Marlborough while the juniors became Earls Spencer. Diana's ancestral credentials were impeccable; she was even related to Sir

Winston Churchill, while her father had continued the family's association with royalty as equerry to King George VI and later to Queen Elizabeth II. If Diana needed any closer attachment to the Royal Family, she could say that her own father had both Queen Mary (wife of George V) and Prince Edward (later King Edward VIII and then Duke of Windsor) as godparents; and Queen Elizabeth II was godmother to Diana's brother, Charles, the present Earl Spencer. The royal roots ran very deep indeed.

Park House had been offered, on lease, to the Fermoy family by George V, and it was where Diana's mother had been born in 1936. Diana was described by her father as a 'perfect physical specimen' – even if she was a girl, not the son and heir he had hoped for. Diana's parents were Viscount Althorp and the former Honourable Frances Ruth Burke Roche, whose mother, Lady Fermoy, had been one of the Queen Mother's ladies-in-waiting, as a Woman of the Bedchamber. Diana's heritage, through both lines, made her perfectly eligible to be a royal bride sometime in the future.

Her mother and father were married on 1 June 1954 in Westminster Abbey, with no fewer than ten members of the Royal Family among the 1,500 guests, including The Queen, Prince Philip, the Queen Mother and Princess Margaret; the ceremony was followed by a reception at St James's Palace. Diana had two older sisters, Sarah, who married a former Coldstream Guards officer, Neil McCorquodale, and Jane, who became the wife of Robert (now Lord) Fellowes, at one time Private Secretary to Her Majesty. Then came a younger brother, Charles, born in 1964, the longed-for heir to the title and estates. Another brother, John, born in 1960, survived only ten hours. Life at Park House was orderly, traditional and aristocratic. The Spencer children lived in the nursery wing on the first floor, set away from the main building, and saw their parents only for an hour in the morning and at teatime, though Diana's mother would occasionally be seen pushing a pram through the parkland surrounding the house.

Childhood playmates included the young princes, Andrew and Edward, who came to swim in the heated pool at Park House so Diana grew up surrounded by members of the Royal Family, young and old. If ever a young girl was comfortable about socialising with royalty, that girl was Diana. Her upbringing subconsciously trained her in the etiquette of the royal court, so it was difficult for some people to understand why she should have felt so uncomfortable when she first became a member of the Royal Family. It wasn't as if she was a complete outsider, unlike Catherine Middleton who came from a family with no royal connections but nevertheless moved seamlessly into royal life. Diana knew the form.

When Diana was six her parents separated and later divorced, the children remaining with their father. Their lives changed dramatically in 1975 when Viscount Althorp succeeded his father as 8th Earl Spencer, Diana becoming Lady Diana, and they moved to the stately home at Althorp (pronounced 'Altrup' by the family) in Northamptonshire. Home to the Spencers since the 16th century, it is a magnificent estate of 15,000 acres; the house itself is a gem, containing over 700 works of art, including original paintings by artists such as Rubens and Constable. While not on the same scale as Buckingham Palace or some of the other royal residences, Althorp was an impressive enough house to grow up in, so Diana was not likely to be overwhelmed when the time came for her to become a future queen-in-waiting.

The year after the move to Althorp, Earl Spencer married Raine, Countess of Dartmouth, whose mother was romantic novelist Barbara Cartland. Raine was not welcomed by the children, including Diana who was away at school for much of the time. She and her siblings had little in common with their new stepmother – they refused to attend the wedding – and they all felt she was trying to take their father away from them and change the way Althorp had been run for centuries. Raine went through the place like a cyclone, altering centuries of tradition and order, and her husband, Johnnie Spencer, gave her her head to do whatever she wished.

From 1974 Diana was a boarder at West Heath School in Kent, where she was said to be an 'average' pupil academically but excellent at sports, particularly swimming. She then went to a finishing school in Switzerland, where she studied domestic science, typing and correspondence, and became fluent in French, as is nearly every member of the Royal Family. She also found plenty of time to enjoy skiing, a sport she would come to indulge in whenever she could.

RIGHT: Lady Diana, aged 13, with her Shetland pony, Soufflé. Although a bad fall, in which she broke her arm, put Diana off horse riding, she later encouraged her sons to ride.

Lady Diana Spencer: Sloane Ranger

When Diana returned to Britain from Switzerland she lived in London, sharing an apartment with old school friends. She moved quite naturally in the society that was described by some as 'Sloane Rangers', so called because much of their leisure time was spent in the fashionable shops and restaurants around the affluent Sloane Square in the Royal Borough of Kensington and Chelsea.

Diana became a nanny to a number of children, and took a three-month cookery course before joining the Young England Kindergarten as a helper. She enjoyed the social whirl of attending parties in the evenings and going to the country at weekends. Diana would stay with friends or occasionally go back to Althorp, where she would visit her sister and brother-in-law, Jane and Robert Fellowes, at their house on the estate.

In July 1980, Diana was invited to join Prince Philip and the rest of the Royal Family, including Prince Charles, on board the Royal Yacht *Britannia* for the Isle of Wight Cowes regatta. She stayed on board for five days and not a single member of the press corps caught sight of her. It was the Royal Family displaying its mastery of how to avoid unwanted attention. It wasn't until September of that same year

that Charles and Diana's relationship was discovered. Diana had been invited to Balmoral, and Arthur Edwards, the most successful newspaper photographer of royals, took an exclusive shot of Charles fishing in the River Dee, with Diana watching from the riverbank. From then on, the media saw her as fair game. Most of Diana's circle of friends came from a similar background, and when her relationship with the Prince of Wales began they automatically provided her with a shield of protection. Once it was suspected that Prince Charles and Lady Diana were romantically involved, news reporters and cameramen pursued her relentlessly. They besieged her flat at Coleherne Court in Knightsbridge, which her father had bought for £50,000 and which today would be worth some 50 times that amount, and followed her everywhere. It was a very testing time for the teenage Diana. She learned to keep her head down, literally, becoming known as 'Shy Di' to journalists. So began the highly intensive media attention which was to continue throughout her life.

At first Diana blushed whenever she was asked by the press about Charles; nobody ever heard her even mention his name in public – even among her friends she was the soul of discretion. And no matter how much the newshounds chased her and her friends, trying to discover a secret boyfriend who might sell them a fresh story or give them the latest gossip about the newest royal interest, they failed, one simple reason being that there *was* nobody to 'kiss-and-tell'. Diana was one of the

LEFT: An English Heritage blue plaque at Coleherne Court, the mansion where Diana had an apartment and was besieged by the paparazzi.

RIGHT: The Prince of Wales and Lady Diana Spencer in the grounds of Buckingham Palace on 24 February 1981, the day of their engagement.

few young women of her class and generation who did not collect admirers along the way and there was no 'significant other' in her teenage years; she certainly was not boy-mad.

At this time Diana was still working at the kindergarten where she was later photographed with two small children. When the photograph was published, it revealed the fact that her skirt was see-through in sunlight, and showing her legs caused the young woman great embarrassment. As she later said, 'I don't want to be remembered for having no petticoat.'

Photographers and reporters appeared wherever she went, and at all hours of the day and night. It is to Diana's credit that she was invariably polite to them – without giving them even a hint of what was to come.

Once her engagement to Prince Charles was official, Diana moved into an apartment in Clarence House, home of the Queen Mother, where she would be protected from the media by the royal press office. Charles had been required, under the Royal Marriages Act of 1772, to seek the permission of The Queen, and also both Houses of Parliament, in order to marry. He would later be forced to go down the same route to have the marriage dissolved.

A Fairy-Tale Royal Wedding

The wedding of the Prince of Wales and Lady Diana Spencer took place at St Paul's Cathedral on 29 July 1981, less than a month after the bride's 20th birthday. It was a day of joy for everyone: the bride and groom, their families and the millions of people watching on television across the globe.

The occasion was a combination of pageantry, high emotion, formal ceremony and vociferous enthusiasm. It was, without doubt, a most wonderful and unforgettable day – and, with an estimated worldwide television audience of 750 million, also the biggest media boost Britain had celebrated since the coronation in 1953. On the eve of the wedding, more than 500,000 people gathered in Hyde Park to witness the royal firework spectacular, with many loyal fans remaining to camp out overnight so they could make sure of the best viewing points when the wedding processions began. As the day of the wedding dawned, the crowds filled every tiny corner and available viewpoint along the two-mile route from Buckingham Palace to St Paul's Cathedral: the police estimated there were at least 600,000 people of all ages and of almost every nationality. The day was designated as a public holiday; a celebratory atmosphere prevailed everywhere – and there were no protests or anti-royalist demonstrations.

Diana was everyone's idea of a fairy-tale bride; her dress, designed by David and Elizabeth Emanuel, was a triumph of ivory silk taffeta, hand embroidered with thousands of tiny mother-of-pearl sequins and pearls, trimmed with sparkling antique lace and with a 25-foot (7.5-metre) train. Diana wore the Spencer family tiara, matched with diamond earrings borrowed from her mother. Accompanied by her father, the bride left Clarence House in the royal Glass Coach to the thunderous cheers of the crowds lining The Mall. At St Paul's Cathedral the groom was waiting, dressed in the uniform of a Royal Navy commander, with a splendid blue sash of the Order of the Garter. Alongside Prince Charles were his two best men (known in the Royal Family as supporters): his brothers, Prince Andrew, at that time a Royal Navy midshipman, and Prince Edward. Seated behind them were the 2,650 guests invited to the wedding, including nearly all the crowned heads of Europe. Among the celebrity guests were Princess Grace of Monaco (the former Hollywood movie star Grace Kelly), accompanied by her son, Prince Albert (now ruler of Monaco.)

From the moment Diana married Charles, the most eligible bachelor in the world at the time, she became not only Princess of Wales but also Countess of Chester, Duchess of Cornwall, Duchess of Rothesay, Countess of Carrick and Baroness of Renfrew – the female equivalents of her husband's subsidiary titles. Little did the new princess, or anyone else, realise that within a decade the fairy-tale would turn into a nightmare.

From that historic day, Diana's life changed forever. She would never again be allowed to wander through Knightsbridge shops and restaurants with her friends. Everything she did would be planned down to the finest detail, with royal protocol and tradition ruling. A police protection officer would be allocated as part of a special team to guard her night and day. She would not even be permitted to drive her own car unaccompanied; a police bodyguard would always have to be at her side.

The wedding presents the couple received numbered over 6,000, including something from almost every monarch and Head of State. President of the United States Ronald Regan was unwell and unable to attend the wedding but Nancy, his First Lady, was a guest and the couple gave a 'Crusader' crystal bowl; Crown Prince Fahd of Saudi Arabia offered a complete set of jewellery that included a diamond watch, rings, earrings and bracelets, with the entire collection estimated to be worth many millions. Men, women and children from every walk of life sent gifts, some handmade and simple, others practical … but there wasn't a single toaster!

After the wedding ceremony the couple returned to Buckingham Palace in the 1902 State Landau, while vast crowds pressed against the railings to catch a glimpse of the new Princess of Wales. After the wedding breakfast, the newly-weds left the palace in a balloon-bedecked carriage. They started their honeymoon at Broadlands, the Hampshire home of the late Lord Mountbatten, Prince Charles's 'honorary grandfather'; they then flew to Gibraltar to join the Royal Yacht *Britannia* for a Mediterranean cruise, and finally joined the Royal Family at Balmoral. Diana later said it was then that she began to realise that her life would never be normal in the usual sense of the word. With the family with them on their honeymoon, something that Charles accepted as quite normal, there was rarely an opportunity for the couple to plan their future together. One might say that having grown up at Althorp in a family who had known royalty for generations, Diana should have been aware of the steps she was taking when she accepted Prince Charles's proposal. But who could have guessed that within a few years cracks in the marriage would appear, and that separation and divorce would follow?

RIGHT: On their honeymoon at Balmoral, the Prince and Princess of Wales share a tender moment beside the River Dee.

LEFT: At Epsom Derby in 1986, Princess Diana chats with her favourite royal relation, her father-in-law, the Duke of Edinburgh.

OPPOSITE: Princess Diana, wearing a chiffon evening gown by Bellville Sassoon, arrives at London's Victoria & Albert Museum on 4 November 1981 for the 'Splendours of the Gonzagas' exhibition gala. The following day came the offical announcement from Buckingham Palace that she was pregnant with her first child.

Princess of Wales: Royal Family Life

From the moment they were married, the Prince and Princess of Wales became the focus of public attention to an extent never before experienced in Britain, even by the Royal Family. They became the most closely watched couple in the world. While Prince Charles was used to being in the spotlight, for Diana it was a new experience but she coped magnificently.

Her early days as Princess of Wales were not easy, however. She was coming to grips with being a working member of the Royal Family, finding ways to impress her own style upon her new homes at Kensington Palace and Highgrove, and also getting used to the idea that she was in the public eye, with very little privacy. For one so young, Diana displayed an extraordinary sense of duty, yet before long she was insistent that her prime role in life was to be a good mother to her children. Charles and Diana became parents in 1982 and when they visited Australia the following year she refused to leave their baby, Prince William, behind, saying she was not going to be separated from him for such a long period and miss what she regarded as an important part of his life. It showed that the princess had a mind of her own and was not prepared to be merely an accessory. And as she grew in

confidence, she also became more demanding, knowing that any request from her was regarded as an order within the Royal Household. Dr Robert Runcie, Archbishop of Canterbury 1980–91, summed up the feelings of a number of those close to her when he said, 'I don't think it's any secret that Diana could be very difficult.' It is clear that from the moment she entered the Royal Family, she took centre stage.

Across the globe, presidents and prime ministers vied with each other in their efforts to persuade the Prince and Princess of Wales to visit them. Politicians of every hue tried every trick in the book to be photographed alongside Diana, knowing that the resulting photograph was likely to feature prominently in newspapers and glossy magazines. Charles had been used to press intrusion all his life. However, nothing he had experienced previously compared with the mass adulation and widespread fascination that Diana attracted wherever they went. And if Prince Charles arrived at a function without his wife at his side, his hosts tried hard not to show their disappointment. Charles quickly began to realise that Diana was the number one attraction and, with wry good humour, he decided to take a back seat saying, 'I know it's my wife you want – not me.' Actually, he was being too modest; although Diana was undoubtedly the new star in the family, Charles himself was still a very popular royal.

The role of Princess of Wales was ill-defined – there was no job description or on-the-job training schedule, so when Diana took on the position she gave it a modern twist, combining glamour with dignity and grace. And it must be remembered that she was still barely out of her teens, being just 20 years old on her wedding day.

Diana may have been born into a family with generations of royal service behind them, yet she was totally unprepared when she was thrust on to the royal scene with all its unwritten rules and regulations. No one told her that for Christmas at Sandringham members of the family were expected to arrive in strict order of seniority, or that all presents between family members were to be cheap and cheerful: the cheaper the better. She was highly embarrassed when her new relatives burst out laughing as they discovered she had gone to enormous trouble and spent a small fortune on her gifts. The joke was on her and she was very upset.

When she began her public duties, Diana found some of them boring in the extreme. When she mentioned this to her father-in-law, Prince Philip (her favourite royal relation), he agreed that some were 'less interesting' than others, displaying

RIGHT: Princess Diana, Prince Charles, The Queen and Prince Philip with British Prime Ministers past and present in 1992. John Major, next to Diana, was Prime Minister at the time. The event was a formal dinner held in Spencer House in London, built in the 18th century for Diana's ancestor, John, 1st Earl Spencer.

unusual discretion and diplomacy in his description, adding that it was the price he and she had to pay for the positions they occupied. Diana summed it up in these words, shortly before her death in 1997: 'I was an outsider and let's face it I never had a chance.'

The House of Windsor is an exclusive club and the most difficult one to join. Would-be candidates cannot apply, they have to wait to be invited. Then they are carefully examined by the existing members and if found to be appropriate, finally they have to be approved by the Chairman of the Board, who in Diana's day was The Queen. Diana was not the only person to find this out the hard way. Others, including Antony Armstrong-Jones (later Lord Snowdon), Sarah Ferguson (now Duchess of York) and Sophie Rhys-Jones (now Countess of Wessex), also discovered what it was like to try and become royal. It was never easy – and sometimes impossible. Lord Snowdon said he always felt like an outsider and that he and Diana were in similar positions regarding the Royal Family. When he, a working photographer, became engaged to The Queen's sister, Princess Margaret, her aunt, Princess Marina, Duchess of Kent, was heard to murmur, 'How strange to be marrying a subject.' This was back in 1960, so attitudes had changed considerably by the time Charles and Diana married in 1981, but Diana and Lord Snowdon often chatted about their relative positions and compared notes in private on their in-laws. One of the things they were agreed upon was that Prince Philip had welcomed them both and went out of his way to make them feel comfortable.

LEFT: In November 1985, on their first visit together to the USA, the Prince and Princess of Wales take tea in the White House with President Ronald Reagan and First Lady Nancy Reagan.

OPPOSITE: Diana looked stunning in a Victor Edelstein dress when she arrived at a Royal Gala Benefit evening in support of the London City Ballet, which took place in Washington DC in October 1990.

Diana's Love Affair with America

For the second time in two centuries the cry went up: 'The British are coming.' But this time it wasn't Paul Revere's famous warning of 18 April 1775 at the start of the War of Independence. This time they were welcome and were there by special invitation.

The British in question were, of course, Charles and Diana – and Diana in particular conquered America with her brilliant combination of charisma coupled with a down-to-earth approach. She fell hopelessly in love with the United States and the nation fell in love with her.

The year was 1985 and even blasé Washingtonians – well accustomed to having world celebrities in their midst – were excited. During an interview I was privileged to have with Diana in 1987, she revealed to me that the visit was the highlight of her entire time as Princess of Wales. The royal couple were welcomed to the White House by President Ronald Reagan and Nancy, the First Lady, surrounded by a symphony of photographers' cameras. For Ronald Reagan, as a former Hollywood movie star, this level of attention was nothing new; he was used to being in the never-ending spotlight of public interest. But for Diana it was, initially, a little

overwhelming, particularly as she was still suffering the effects of jet lag after the long flight.

The first and most exciting of the banquets Charles and Diana attended during that visit took place in the White House on the evening of 9 November. After once again posing for the obligatory photographs – this time in formal wear – the host and hostess and their principal guests made their way into the ballroom where the other guests were seated at tables of ten.

After dinner the party moved into the magnificent East Room, the American version of a Royal State Apartment, where Diana was thrilled to be serenaded by Neil Diamond. She had requested his presence and the song 'You Don't Bring Me Flowers'; the singer, the song and indeed the entire guest list had been approved by both the White House and the Royal Household beforehand. This was one party where it was impossible to buy your way in.

Neil Diamond then claimed his singer's prerogative by dancing with Diana before another famous personality claimed the next dance; this privilege went to the actor Tom Selleck, who at 6 feet 4 inches (1.93 metres) was able to tower over his dance partner – even though she was 5 feet 10 inches (1.77 metres).

Hollywood royalty was present in force that evening. Diana said that she nearly swooned when film actor and director Clint Eastwood took to the dance floor with her – and Prince Charles did not look at all pleased. Diana was delighted that at this event she could dance wearing her favourite high heels – which she could not do when out with Charles, who was slightly shorter than his wife.

Ronald Reagan showed that he too was no slouch on the dance floor when he claimed the host's privilege of partnering the young princess in a slow foxtrot. He later said that Diana was so beautiful and elegant she could have graced the red carpet at the Hollywood Oscars just as much as a State banquet.

But the pair all eyes were on came next, when John Travolta led Diana on to the floor. Actor and singer Travolta wasn't sure what the etiquette was, not knowing whether he should approach Diana and ask her to dance or wait to be asked by Her Royal Highness. In fact, Diana had already let it be known that there was nobody she wanted to dance with more than Travolta, ever since she had seen him in *Grease*. In her sitting room at Kensington Palace, she told me that when she watched the movie she fantasised about playing the part filled by Olivia Newton-John; now she could – and did – and the sensational images were broadcast all around the world.

The fun of Diana's first trip to America was balanced with more serious discussions. She and Nancy Reagan found common ground in their charity work and, through that relationship, on at least two later occasions Diana helped the American Red Cross: in 1994 when she made a private visit to their headquarters; and in 1997 when she delivered a speech in Washington DC supporting their landmine campaign.

Diana developed a love for America and Americans in general; after that 1985 trip she was to make a number of further visits on her own, often staying at one of

RIGHT: Everyone was eager to meet Princess Diana when she arrived at Harlem Hospital in 1989.

New York's most famous hotels, The Carlyle. Her first solo trip – and indeed her first ever visit to New York – was on 1 February 1989. As she stepped off Concorde at John F. Kennedy Airport, she was there in an official capacity to promote British trade in the USA, but, of course, the social scene was also high on the agenda, with cocktail parties attracting the great and good of the city. During that visit, she made history when she visited Harlem Hospital in New York and comforted children stricken with AIDS, and later dropped in to the famous toy store FAO Schwarz to see how British toys were selling. After that first visit to New York, it held a special place in her heart; she adored the city with which she established a loving and substantial relationship.

Diana was to meet many US presidents during her lifetime. The British Royal Family has long had a close association with the people who have served in that role, some of whom have become personal friends. President George Bush senior knew The Queen for many years and he stayed at Buckingham Palace, both when he was president and in a private capacity. Diana was delighted to meet him and his First Lady, Barbara Bush, several times. Like Nancy Reagan, Mrs Bush and Diana had a shared interest in charity work and in October 1990 the princess was invited to the White House, where over coffee she and the First Lady discussed their mutual concern for those suffering from AIDS.

In 1995, while separated from Prince Charles, Diana was again a solo traveller to the United States. She attended the 14th Annual Fashion Designers of America

LEFT: Diana and Barbara Bush at the White House in 1990.

Awards Gala in New York on 30 January, when for once she didn't stand out as she might have wished; she had just had her hair washed and decided to keep the wet look which many people felt was not the most attractive style for her.

In December that year, she flew to New York by Concorde to attend a charity event, where she was accompanied by distinguished US statesmen Henry Kissinger and Colin Powell. As soon as the news that Diana was attending got round, the $2,000 tickets sold out in hours. Among the 850 dinner guests were New York's former mayor Ed Koch, and human rights activist Bianca Jagger. Diana was particularly pleased to meet the woman termed 'America's first lady of television', Barbara Walters. Miss Walters is remembered for, in 1976, being the first woman on television to be paid $1 million a year; today her salary would be nearer to $20 million.

As with every royal visit, both at home or abroad, there were certain rules laid down in advance of meeting Diana: how to address the princess, whether one should bow or curtsey to her (the answer being 'no'), and in particular her likes and dislikes regarding food and drink. The main food guidelines were very simple: no garlic and no onions.

On a triumphant three-day visit to Chicago in June 1996, to help raise funds for cancer research, Diana did the now expected walkabout. There was nothing she

LEFT: In December 1995, Diana was named Humanitarian of the Year and presented with an award by Henry Kissinger, former US Secretary of State, on behalf of the United Cerebral Palsy charity in recognition of her work with sick and underprivileged children. At the gala event, which raised over £2 million for the charity, Diana spoke of the need to demonstrate compassion, saying, 'Let us not wait to be asked.'

liked more than meeting people from all walks of life in as informal a manner as was possible for someone in her position. In the United States, although security was clearly a high priority, she was able to talk and shake hands with hundreds of young men and women of her own age. It is perhaps fortunate that the age of the 'selfie' had not arrived or she would never have got away from all those who wanted to have a photograph taken with her.

Chicago's Northwestern University was thrilled to welcome its most royal visitor. Hundreds of well-wishers greeted Diana's arrival in a black Rolls-Royce when she drew up at the university's Weber Arch before joining the governor of Illinois and the mayors of Chicago and Evanston and their spouses at a reception hosted by Northwestern's president, Henry Biensen. Diana gave the opening remarks at a symposium on breast cancer and Biensen later stated: 'No other woman has the ability to so effectively focus the world's attention on such critical issues.'

On a lighter note, the Princess of Wales was also guest of honour at a black-tie gala at Chicago's Field Museum of Natural History, where she wore a floor-length Versace gown, and danced with famed television host Phil Donohue. Tony Bennett serenaded Diana, and the A-list guests included basketball player Michael Jordan's mother, Deloris, who presented Diana with autographed Chicago Bulls souvenirs for Princes William and Harry. As Diana boarded her flight to return to London she said, 'I love Chicago. It's been wonderful.' And the trip was also a financial success, raising $1.3 million for cancer research.

In June 1997, Diana was again in New York. She met the journalist Tina Brown for luncheon at the iconic Four Seasons restaurant, with the main purpose of her visit being to attend the charity auction of 79 of her own dresses at the Park Avenue salesroom of Christie's. Among the guests Diana was delighted to meet once again was distinguished television journalist Barbara Walters. The auction raised some $3.25 million for charities. Sadly, this was to be Diana's last visit to the USA; less than three months later, she had died.

Earlier that year, Diana had joined Hillary Clinton at the White House; America's First Lady had persuaded the princess to help with one of her charities dealing with breast cancer. The two of them attended a breakfast meeting and, as we now know, Hillary Clinton travelled across the Atlantic that September to attend the funeral of her friend Diana at Westminster Abbey.

During her many visits to the United States, Diana's popularity never waned and she continued to be treated as royalty. Americans saw her as both an innocent victim and a winner in the divorce battle, and acclaimed her as a great survivor and a successful single mother. After she returned from her first visit to the USA, and in spite of the fact that she was Princess of Wales, a very important title in Britain, she said, respectfully, she would have loved, in another world, to be First Lady of America.

RIGHT: One of Diana's dresses by Catherine Walker on display at Christie's in preparation for the charity auction in June 1997. The princess had worn the burgundy velvet dress, with matching embroidered jacket, to a film premiere in London's Leicester Square in 1990.

Princess of Style, Beauty and Grace

It was Diana's first change in hairstyle that seemed to transform her the most. Soon after her wedding, her pageboy cut was replaced by a new, fuller style. Sophisticated and totally stunning, what was termed 'the Diana look' had arrived and a new photographic image was created.

It was not just her hairstyles that caused interest and comment in newspapers and magazines. If ever a person could justifiably claim to be a one-woman fashion industry, that person must have been Diana, Princess of Wales. Almost single-handedly she rejuvenated the British fashion scene, practically from the moment she first stepped on to the royal stage.

She was acclaimed as one of the best-dressed women in the world and to the younger generation she was the number one style-setter. Yet she was heard to say on more than one occasion, 'Clothes are not my priority. I enjoy bright colours … but fashion isn't my big thing at all.' Hardly the words one would expect to hear from someone who was said to possess 200 pairs of shoes and 300 pairs of earrings, and whose wardrobe filled two full-size rooms at Kensington Palace with evening dresses, ball gowns, casual outfits and a wide variety of day wear.

Because of her height and slim figure, Diana could show off almost any outfit to its best advantage. Legions of women, from Japan to Jersey, faithfully copied her style down to the tiniest detail. When she appeared in a 'Robin Hood' style hat in the early 1980s, identical copies were bought in their thousands; and when she wore, somewhat mischievously, a diamond necklace as a headband, jewellers worldwide were inundated the next day with enquiries for replicas. Diana never saw herself as a fashion icon and she disliked the description, believing it detracted from her more serious side. She said she never followed fashion, only dressing 'for the job in hand'. The truth is she was not a follower of fashion but a trendsetter, and if she was set up as an icon it was only because others admired her innate sense of style and her ability to choose what was right for her. She combined, with great success, a modern look with the requirements of royal dignity and cool elegance.

The demands of her position necessitated a large wardrobe, and Diana was determined to showcase the very best of British design and manufacture wherever she went on her overseas tours, performing an extraordinary service for the fashion industry, and bringing a new and glamorous image to the Royal Family. She knew instinctively what suited her. But, more importantly, she knew how to adapt outfits both to her own personality and the day-to-day needs of the job. When she was carrying out public duties, either as a member of the Royal Family or later as a private person, whatever she wore on those occasions had to be suitable for getting in and out of cars and aeroplanes with dignity. Many of her days were long and tiring but she had to look as fresh in the evening as she had first thing in the morning, so crease-resistant clothes were the order of the day.

Among Diana's favourite fashion houses from the 1980s onwards were Bruce Oldfield and Catherine Walker. She was not dressed exclusively by British designers, however. The princess was also seen, especially in later years, in outfits by Christian Dior, John Galliano, Gianni Versace and Jacques Azagury.

Diana never hid the fact that one of the advantages of being royal was that she could get to meet just about anyone she wanted. She was fascinated by show business and the arts, and missed no opportunity to mix with stars of stage and screen: dancers, singers and actors. She got on famously with singer Michael Jackson and said he even taught her how to do his famous 'Moonwalk' dance.

Dancing was a great love of hers, and in particular ballet. As patron of the English National Ballet she played an active role in the organisation, often turning up to watch rehearsals and staying behind to talk with the dancers. She once wistfully remarked that she would have loved to have been a ballet dancer but 'at 5 feet 10 inches I'm too tall' – so when she sprang a surprise Christmas present on Prince Charles in 1985 by dancing on stage with Wayne Sleep at the Royal Opera House, she was also achieving a lifetime ambition. Some years previously, when she partnered John Travolta on the dance floor at the White House in Washington DC, both Diana and Travolta said it was a 'dream come true'.

It was in response to a suggestion by Prince William that in June 1997 Diana assigned Christie's in New York to auction 79 of her dresses in an event that raised $3.25million (today equivalent to around £2.5 million) for charities. The garments ranged from short cocktail dresses to formal ball gowns and included her favourite: a Victor Edelstein creation in duchesse satin with matching bolero jacket, which sold for $90,500 (approximately £70,000 today). Among Diana's charities, for whom she worked indefatigably, was the Royal Marsden Hospital Cancer Fund and she insisted that part of the proceeds of the auction should go to the hospital. The rest of the money went to another of her favourite causes, the AIDS Crisis Trust.

RIGHT: Even after her death, Diana was gracing the covers of magazines, as shown on this special edition of *Life* magazine in November 1997.

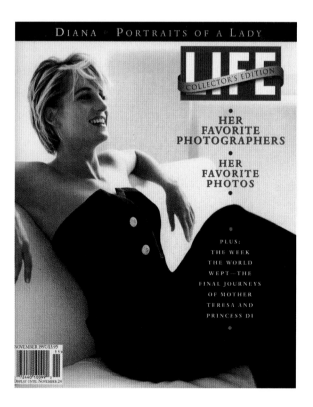

Diana: The Real Princess of Wales

From the day in 1981 that she married Charles, Prince of Wales, Diana was determined to become a real Princess of Wales, not merely one in name only. She refused to accept that hers was simply a titular role. She set out to learn everything she could about the country whose name she bore and also to meet as many of its people as she could.

Diana had first visited Wales shortly after her wedding in 1981 as part of what was termed the 'honeymoon tour' of the United Kingdom. It was in October of that year that she was made a Freeman of the City of Cardiff, making a short speech in Welsh for which she received a round of applause for her valiant efforts. It was obvious that she was very nervous but the people of Wales took her to their hearts immediately and it became obvious that the feeling was mutual. She never tired of visiting Wales and once said she would have loved to have had a home in the Principality; it was not until 2006 that Prince Charles bought a house in Llandovery in Mid Wales. Diana also asked jokingly if it was true that as a Freeman of Cardiff she was permitted to drive her sheep through the city's streets. Apparently, it was once one of the privileges!

On 13 February 1990, she visited the hospital named after her in South Wales, the Princess of Wales Hospital in Bridgend, and she invited me to join her, even sending an official car to collect me from my home. When we arrived hundreds of people were waiting to greet her; it seemed that nearly every one of them was carrying a bunch of flowers that they wanted to give her. She waved and called out that she would talk to them later. When the visit was ending, after running over two hours late due to her wanting to meet as many people as she could, Diana emerged to find the crowds still waiting patiently. In spite of being urged to hurry by the officials, she walked over to them and chatted for half an hour. As we travelled back to Cardiff Airport she said, 'If they can wait for two hours for me, I can certainly spend half an hour with them.' One of the cars in the motorcade was packed with the flowers she had been given and before she left to return to London she told the airport workers, cleaners, security staff and police to each take a bouquet and give it to '… your sweetheart, wife, girlfriend or mother tomorrow with my love. Because don't forget, tomorrow is St Valentine's Day.' It is difficult to imagine any other member of the Royal Family doing or saying such a thing.

It was on 1 March 1991 – St David's Day, Wales's national day – that Diana took Prince William to Cardiff for the first time. It was on this occasion that William, signing the visitors' book at the city's Llandaff Cathedral, revealed that he is left-handed. This was the same year that Diana took Prince Harry to Cardiff Arms Park to see the Wales v. Australia international rugby match, and where she joined in singing the national anthem – in Welsh! She later said that one of her proudest moments was when she was told she had been adopted as the 'unofficial mascot' of the Welsh team.

Tŷ Hafan is a charity hospice in South Wales that provides, in comfortable surroundings, holistic, palliative care for children with life-limiting conditions. It was one of the many causes Diana championed in Wales, and in 1995 she attended a concert at Cardiff International Arena by Luciano Pavarotti that raised thousands of pounds for the charity. Signor Pavarotti later said that Diana's presence could change even the most ordinary event into a spectacular occasion.

Like many other nations, Wales warmed to Diana. The Welsh welcomed her as 'one of us'; her lack of airs and graces, her vulnerable side and ability to show her emotions saw them springing to her defence. And being loved for what she was, not who she was, was very important to Diana.

RIGHT: October 1991: Prince Harry stands alongside his mother as she joins in the singing of the Welsh national anthem at Cardiff Arms Park.

LEFT: The christening of Prince William took place at Buckingham Palace on 4 August 1982. With the baby and his parents are his godparents (known as sponsors in royal circles): ex-King Constantine of Greece (seated); standing (left to right) Princess Alexandra, Lord Romsey, Lady Hussey, Sir Laurens Van Der Post and the Duchess of Westminster.

OPPOSITE: Fun with her youngest son! Diana with Prince Harry at Thorpe Park, Surrey in 1992. She and her boys visited the theme park several times and she always insisted they queue for the rides and be treated like everybody else.

A Devoted Mother

The most important role in Diana's life was motherhood. She had always had a special affinity with children and never doubted for a moment that she was intended to be a mother. Speaking about her children, she once said of them, 'They mean everything to me'; she later added, 'I always feed my children love and affection – it's so important.'

Although their marriage ended in divorce, there were many times when the Prince and Princess of Wales enjoyed great happiness together. One such moment was at 9.03pm on 21 June 1982, when Diana gave birth to her first son, Prince William Arthur Philip Louis, in the private Lindo Wing of St Mary's Hospital in London. Prince Charles broke with royal tradition by being present at the birth, and it was also the first time that an heir apparent had been born in hospital. Both Diana and Prince Charles were overjoyed.

They were loving, affectionate parents and Diana said she had found her true destiny. She was never happier than when she was playing with William, whom she called Wills. Two years later her second child, Prince Harry, was born. And although there was an acrimonious divorce some years later, both Charles and Diana were

always agreed on the welfare of their children. They both adored William and Harry, and there was never a problem concerning how they should be brought up and of their futures; everything else was secondary. And, had she lived, Diana would have been a proud and loving mother-in-law to Catherine and Meghan, and a devoted grandmother to George, Charlotte, Louis, Archie and Lilibet.

Off duty, Diana would attempt to shrug off rigid royal protocol and relax with her sons. She was determined that, although they would never forget who they were, they should have as normal an upbringing as possible. She took them to the cinema, letting them choose the films they wanted to see, and introduced them to the delights of fast-food hamburger restaurants, where she queued with other parents. She was a thoroughly modern mother who refused to allow her royal role to interfere with the ordinary, everyday joys of bringing up her children. Diana turned up at the boys' annual sports days, kicked off her shoes and ran barefoot in the mothers' race – which, memorably, she won in 1991, to her sons' great delight.

When the time came for Prince William to go away to school, Diana expressed a very clear preference for Eton. Prince Charles was more than happy to agree with that preference. He had been educated at Gordonstoun in Scotland at the insistence

LEFT: Like so many royal babies before him, Prince Harry wore the Honiton lace christening gown when he was baptised at St George's Chapel, Windsor Castle in December 1984; the garment was first worn by Queen Victoria's eldest child in 1841.

of his father, Prince Philip, but hated every moment of his time there. Diana chose Eton because it was near enough to London that she could see her son frequently, while allowing him to become a boarder like his peers. Both of William's parents insisted that he should be treated the same as the other pupils.

Diana impressed upon both of her sons their connection with the Principality, whose name they shared, telling them never to forget what they were: Prince William and Prince Harry of Wales. She instilled in the boys her own sense of public awareness from an early age, and showed them, at first hand, how the underprivileged are forced to live by taking them with her to The Passage, a centre for the homeless near Westminster Cathedral in London. Their first visit, in 1993, was a salutary experience for the young princes, but one which she felt was necessary in their ongoing training for their later roles.

Diana is remembered in many different ways, but undoubtedly the most important legacy of her extraordinary life is her two sons. Inevitably, most of the attention has been on Prince William, now the Prince of Wales and King Charles III's heir to the throne. Sometime this century, Prince William (who on the day he married was created Duke of Cambridge) will be crowned King William V, or whatever regnal name he chooses. It is an inevitable situation that William would

not change even if he could. Reports that King Charles III might have stepped aside in favour of his elder son were based on pure speculation. The Prince of Wales will, eventually, follow his father as king. The late Lord Blake, one of Britain's foremost authorities on the monarchy and the constitution, once said, 'Charles's whole life has been geared to the assumption that he will be king. There is not the slightest evidence from anyone that he has any intention of giving it up. And even if he wanted to turn the throne over to William, the choice of succession is not his to make. Parliament would have to agree to allow Charles to leave, then select a new king, and that could throw the entire idea of monarchy open to official and possibly acrimonious debate.' Such debates are now unnecessary, of course, since Charles became monarch following the death of his mother in September 2022.

Although much focus was placed on William as future king, Diana was determined that her second child would never feel an outsider. Prince Henry Charles Albert David, always known as Harry, was born on 15 September 1984, in the same hospital as his brother two years previously. Harry is a typical second son in that he has known from an early age that he is bound to be a 'tail-end Charlie'. Despite his place in the royal line of succession, Harry will never reach the heights reserved for William. Princess Anne was in a similar position with her older brother, Charles. However, in adulthood Harry has made it clear that he was glad to be the second son, as being monarch is not a role he would ever have wished for.

Diana, of course, never showed any favouritism towards William; in fact, Harry received perhaps a little more attention from her. And it is almost certain that, when Harry left Eton College, she would have approved of and encouraged his decision to take a gap year in which he travelled to Australia and Lesotho. He went on to complete officer training at the Royal Military Academy Sandhurst and during his army career served two tours in Afghanistan, at the time one of the worst trouble spots on the planet.

In his youth, the party-loving Harry made the occasional faux pas that hit the headlines and embarrassed his family but his involvement with charities, including Sentebale and the Invictus Games that he set up, brought him into the public eye for all the right reasons.

Prince Harry became a Counsellor of State when he reached the age of 21. However, his role within the Royal Family changed shortly after his 2018 marriage to Meghan Markle.

RIGHT: The Prince and Princess of Wales presented a united front when they, along with Harry, brought William to Eton College the day before he became a student there in September 1995.

Prince William: King-in-Training

William, above all of his contemporaries, knows exactly what his destiny is: he is going to be king. There is no other role for him.

He was allowed to join the Royal Air Force and to work as an air-ambulance pilot; he also spent time in Africa, on activities relating to various charities with which he is associated. All such involvements were strictly supervised, the people with whom he worked specially chosen, and every aspect of his career had, and continues to have, but one solitary aim: to make him suitable as a future sovereign. His father had the same ongoing training as a king-in-waiting for over 70 years, and his grandmother, Queen Elizabeth II, knew from the age of ten, when her uncle, King Edward VIII, abdicated in 1936 and her father was suddenly propelled into the limelight, from being the comparatively obscure Duke of York to ascending the throne as King George VI, that she too had no control over her destiny. She was heir presumptive and accepted without question that she would become queen – as long as no son had been born to the king and queen, who would have taken precedent even if he were younger. There was no alternative, and where royalty is concerned things haven't changed all that much in the last 200 years – although, significantly,

the 2013 Succession to the Crown Act does mean younger sons can no longer displace elder daughters in the royal line of succession.

The hereditary principle being what it is, Prince William knows that, barring accidents, he will become His Majesty King William V. The last monarch to bear the name was William IV, the third son of George III, who came to the throne at the age of 64 in 1830. Neither father nor son was particularly successful as sovereign. George III is remembered as the king who gave away the American colonies – and for his supposed madness. William IV was often called 'Silly Billy' because of his spontaneous promotions in the Royal Navy in his role as Lord High Admiral; a more respectful and affectionate nickname was the 'Sailor King'.

When he takes the throne, William V may not have a very high standard to live up to in terms of his namesake predecessor, but this William is far different from his ancestors; his training will have prepared him to rule in modern times where the monarch's word is no longer law. Although he will be expected to use the royal prerogative, he already knows that, like his grandmother and father before him, he will be required to work within the rules of democracy. Like them, he will understand that his influence may be massive but his actual power limited. He can have few illusions about his role and the course his life will take.

At a time when the monarchy is being criticised from many sides and when some countries within the Commonwealth – traditionally supportive of having the British sovereign as their Head of State – are turning towards republicanism, William might be excused for questioning whether he will eventually inherit the throne. Indeed will there still be a throne to occupy when his time comes? And how much support will there be for a monarchy, even in Britain, in ten or 20 years from now? William is an intelligent man with an enquiring mind, so these questions must already have cropped up. He will most likely have discussed the problems many times with his father and grandmother. She fully believed in the continuity of the monarchy and had an unshakeable faith that her role and that of her heirs will survive whatever upheavals may follow in the years to come. Others are not so sanguine.

William has shown that he is an independent person who likes to make his own decisions, although this is a trait that royalty discourages. Palace courtiers have noticed his tendency to speak his mind and some fear that his independent streak shows more than a hint of the temperament he has inherited from his mother. They remember the problems Diana caused the Royal Family at times and some sense there could be potential problems later from her eldest son.

RIGHT: Left to right: Prince Charles, Prince Harry, Earl Spencer, Prince William and Prince Philip enter Westminster Abbey, walking behind the coffin bearing Diana, Princess of Wales, 6 September 1997.

In many ways William is an ordinary person who has found himself in an extraordinary situation, unique even. No one else of his generation has had to make the transition from royal splendour, living in palaces and castles, to being just one of 6,000 students at a provincial university. He was also the only student at his, or any other, university (with the possible exception of former President Clinton's daughter, Chelsea) who was required to wear an electronic 'panic button' at all times.

From time to time, William still faces problems in coming to terms with being a member of a family whose every peccadillo is chronicled in minute detail. He carries the ingrained royal suspicion of being exploited and goes out of his way to avoid the possibility. He claims his mother was exploited by many and that her image still is.

'The one thing his father and I were absolutely agreed on was that William would have as normal an upbringing as possible': the words of the late Diana, Princess of Wales, speaking about her first child. It was an understandable and commendable wish but 'normal' is a description that is difficult to quantify when applied to almost any member of the Royal Family, particularly when it concerns someone on whom so many hopes are pinned. William is the shining light of the kingship to come, whom The Queen fully believed will one day take the monarchy safely into the years ahead. And what can be normal when you realise that this particular son cannot fly in the same aircraft as his father in case an accident should deprive the nation of the sovereign and his heir? Or that when he first started at nursery school William wasn't allowed to know its name 'for security reasons', which must have seemed a mystery to the little three-year-old pupil? Even then, as now, almost his every movement has been controlled by royal convention.

LEFT: Before going to university, Prince William spent part of a gap year in Chile with the Operation Raleigh International expedition. One of the projects he helped with was constructing walkways linking parts of the remote village of Tortel.

RIGHT: Prince William graduated from St Andrew's University in June 2005 with a 2:1 in geography. Among other members of his family joining him for the event was his father, Prince Charles, and stepmother, the Duchess of Cornwall, who had married two months previously.

Few other schoolboys have had to bear the burden that Prince William faced at the age of 15: losing his world-famous mother in a horrific car crash; a father involved in what was arguably the most publicised love affair of the century; a grandmother who was also his Queen; and a great-grandfather who was the last Emperor of India. William has never been able to take off and spend a couple of days – or even hours – alone, without informing his police 'minders' where he is going. So 'normal' is not the word that springs to mind when describing his background and life so far.

Keenly aware of his position in the royal line-up, the apparently shy and sometimes introspective Prince William remains what most people regard as the classic first child and older brother. He liked being the one to look out for Harry and, after the death of their mother, regarded himself as the one to whom his younger sibling could look for unqualified support.

Despite their differences in more recent years, there cannot fail to be a common bond between the two men; growing up as part of the Royal Family, each knows better than anyone else the problems the other has had to face. It has long been said that Harry is the more easy-going of the two. He is unlikely ever to have to face the responsibilities of William but has occasionally shown his frustration at living in his brother's shadow. But William enjoys his position and his brother is in no doubt about who is number one.

William has a self-deprecating sense of fun that comes to the fore among his friends and family but he has at times shown a more caustic side towards the press. He inherited many of the characteristics of his grandfather, Prince Philip, including a love of sport, particularly riding and shooting – though he obeyed his mother when she advised him, with an eye on political correctness, not to be photographed holding a shotgun in his hands. And just like Prince Philip (and the Princess Royal), William has a quick temper and does not suffer fools gladly, his short fuse sometimes directed towards photographers. He also follows King Charles III in the manner in which he likes his life to be ordered and planned, accepting without question the deference of royal servants.

William's physical resemblance to his mother is uncanny, with his height, his fair hair and blue eyes all coming from the Spencer family. His character, however, is, in the main, very much the product of the House of Windsor: he is royal through and through.

Perhaps the most poignant image anyone has had of William was at the funeral of his mother in 1997. Walking with his brother Harry and Diana's brother Earl Spencer, their eyes cast down, while Prince Charles and the Duke of Edinburgh held their heads high, few could fail to have been moved as the young princes kept their emotions firmly under control. Their bearing was impeccable and showed a maturity way beyond their years. It was an exercise in royal discipline that William had learned from an early age and one that he will remember all his life. He has long been fully aware that, as heir to the throne, his future is one dictated by public duty and the expectations of an affectionate but demanding people.

OPPOSITE: Prince William at RAF Cranwell in Lincolnshire in April 2008, the day he was presented with his pilot's wings by Prince Charles.

RIGHT: Prince William first visited The Passage, a homeless charity based at the St Vincent's Centre in London, with his mother and brother in 1993. Since then he has visited many times; now its royal patron, he is seen here in September 2021 attending an awards ceremony there.

William and Catherine

The new Prince and Princess of Wales, William and Catherine, or Kate as she is still referred to by many throughout the world, are the perfect example of a young generation that proves one's origins do not matter when love is involved.

Catherine's family, the Middletons, could be described as the face of modern Britain – hard-working, self-made and entrepreneurial: a middle-class family who have successfully bridged the gap between their modest origins and royalty.

Diana would have welcomed Catherine into the family with open arms. As a woman with no class prejudices – or indeed any other kind – Diana would have had no concerns at the working-class background of her daughter-in-law's parents. The fact that they worked hard to enable their children to benefit from first-class educations would have been a plus in her eyes. And when the Middletons welcomed William into their home (albeit a mansion worth over £5 million), Diana would have thoroughly approved of her elder son being given a taste of 'normal' family life.

William and Catherine are the products of prestigious public schools – Eton and Marlborough – and an equally exclusive university, St Andrews, where each obtained a respectable upper second-class degree.

Since their wedding on 29 April 2011 at Westminster Abbey, seen by many as the most prestigious social event of the decade, the couple have captured the attention of the public in a way not seen since Princess Diana first arrived on the royal scene. The manner in which William and Catherine – made Duke and Duchess of Cambridge on their wedding day – accomplished this is in complete contrast to the times when the reverential image of royalty meant that even their names would have been whispered in hushed tones. William, with his undoubted charm and sense of humour, and Catherine, whose beauty and personality make her a photographer's dream, generate an impression of royalty that is a formidable combination of star quality and an approachable common touch, so reminiscent of Diana.

Although it is impossible to forget who Prince William is and what he represents, he has been able to develop an independence formerly unknown among royals: choosing his own friends, meeting people from all walks of life informally, even comparatively trivial things such as visiting restaurants and theatres. He is the most senior member of the Royal Family who has been able to enjoy the company of ordinary people in a manner his father would have found somewhat uncomfortable.

However, Charles was delighted with his elder son's choice of bride and The Queen was equally pleased to welcome Catherine into the fold.

Catherine's background being different to that of her husband has been an enormous advantage. Her stable family gave him an early glimpse of a life that would otherwise have been entirely foreign to him.

Catherine has brought to the Royal Family an easy-going charm that disarms everyone meeting her for the first time. William has said many times that he recognised this quality in Catherine from day one. Another thing he has always found attractive in his wife is their shared sense of humour. One example is that they laugh about the fact that even though they were both born in 1982 (Catherine in January and William in June), she likes to remind him that she is the older – even if only by five months – and will occasionally call him her 'toy boy'.

William and Catherine's engagement was announced on 16 November 2010. Their first official duty together was in February 2011, two months before they were married, when they named a new lifeboat on the isle of Anglesey in North Wales, where William was based at RAF Valley as a helicopter pilot. The following day they travelled to the place they first met, St Andrews University, where William was patron of his old college's 600th anniversary appeal. Catherine was receiving her first taste of what it was going to be like for the rest of her life as in March the couple crossed the Irish Sea to make another official visit, this time to Northern Ireland.

Had Diana still been alive, she would have been the first person to offer any advice and encouragement Catherine may have needed in those early days. As it

RIGHT: The Duke and Duchess of Cambridge, as they were then titled, were at Singapore's National Orchid Garden in September 2012 – part of a tour of the Far East and South Pacific in honour of Queen Elizabeth II's Diamond Jubilee – when they were shown this orchid named 'Dendrobium Memoria Princess Diana', in memory of William's mother.

happened, if appearances are anything to go by, Catherine was perfectly capable of adapting to the rigours of a formal royal routine on her own – well, perhaps with a little help from the man she was about the marry. She moved seamlessly into the role as the young, elegant and beautiful newest member of the most famous family in the world.

William and Catherine, who in September 2022 became Prince and Princess of Wales, are the contemporary face of royalty. When the time comes for William to ascend the throne, they will ensure the continued stability of the British monarchy. In the meantime, together with their three children – Prince George, Princess Charlotte and Prince Louis – they hope to be able to enjoy many years of family life.

Their children, who are second, third and fourth in line of succession to the British throne, were born in St Mary's Hospital in Paddington, London, just like their father and uncle. Despite the exclusivity of the private Lindo Wing of the hospital, one can image our king's great-great-great-grandmother, Queen Victoria, being shocked at the thought of any of her illustrious descendants not being born in a palace or castle – or at least, a royal residence. All of Victoria's nine babies (four sons, five daughters) were delivered in either Buckingham Palace or Windsor Castle.

LEFT: The Duke and Duchess of Cambridge, Prince George, Princess Charlotte and Prince Louis arriving at the London Palladium to enjoy a pantomime in December 2020.

RIGHT: How thrilled Diana would have been to see the Duke and Duchess of Cambridge following her style and engaging closely with the public when they went walkabout in Abergavenny, Monmouthshire on St David's Day 2022.

RIGHT: How thrilled Diana would have been to see the Duke and Duchess of Cambridge following her style and engaging closely with the public when they went walkabout in Abergavenny, Monmouthshire on St David's Day 2022.

Still, how many babies have the honour of being greeted with a military gun salute to mark the occasion? When Prince George was born in 2013, and Princess Charlotte and Prince Louis in 2015 and 2018 respectively, the King's Troop Royal Horse Artillery (still called that, even though our sovereign at the time was a queen) fired a 41-gun salute in Green Park, across the road from Buckingham Palace; the basic salute is 21 rounds but because Green Park is designated a Royal Park an extra 20 rounds were fired. At the same time, an even longer salute was fired at the Tower of London: 62 rounds comprising the basic 21, a further 20 because the Tower of London is a Royal Palace and another 21 because it is in the City of London. Although none of the infants would have been aware of the noisy celebrations, people throughout London heard the guns clearly and knew that a royal birth had taken place. To add to the gaiety, the Union Flag was flown on all government buildings throughout the United Kingdom, on all ships of the Royal Navy and on every defence establishment.

William, Catherine and their children are priceless assets for the future of the monarchy – and for Britain.

Harry and Meghan

History was made on the day Meghan Markle married Prince Harry. She was the first person of mixed-race heritage to join the Royal Family, but not the first American divorcee. That milestone was claimed by the twice-divorced Mrs Wallis Simpson in 1937, when she married the Duke of Windsor, the former King Edward VIII, who abdicated the throne in order to marry her.

Would Diana have welcomed Meghan into the fold? Yes, undoubtedly; Harry's choice of bride would have met with her unqualified agreement. Race and creed did not concern her. Everyone was equal in her eyes. She might also have agreed with their later decision to leave the United Kingdom to live permanently in the United States, a country she adored. However, it is unlikely that she would have supported Harry and Meghan's arguments against the Royal Family, particularly coming at a time when The Queen could have done with all the help the younger members of her family could have provided. Harry and Meghan held such promise, both for the country and for the monarchy. Diana, for all her faults and despite her own problems with the Royal Family, never deserted the country of her birth, even if she did once appear to question the institution of the monarchy during that unfortunate television interview.

The wedding of His Royal Highness Prince Henry Charles Albert David of Wales to his American fiancée Meghan Markle was a royal event with international overtones and more than a touch of glamour and glitz; it was also a rather democratic occasion with all the elements intertwining perfectly.

The 15th-century St George's Chapel at Windsor Castle is one of the finest ecclesiastical buildings in the land. It has been the venue for countless State and royal ceremonies over the centuries: christenings, marriages and funerals of kings, queens, princes and princesses, including the baptism of Prince Harry in 1984, and, significantly, the annual service for the Most Noble Order of the Garter, the oldest and most senior Order of Chivalry in the land. On 19 May 2018, another glittering and memorable chapter was added to this historic and illustrious list.

The marriage service for Harry and Meghan – who had a small piece of fabric from Diana's wedding dress sewn into her own dress for the occasion – was performed by the Archbishop of Canterbury, Justin Welby. The traditional wedding was also noted for its inclusions of African-American culture. An American preacher gave the sermon, which was characterised by its length. On the day of the wedding, The Queen created Harry Duke of Sussex with several subsidiary titles, so that same day Meghan became Her Royal Highness the Duchess of Sussex, Countess of Dumbarton and Baroness of Kilkeel. The transformation from *Suits* star to royalty was complete. It was a magical moment. The American dream come true. Every one of the 600 or so guests inside the chapel was fully appreciative of the grandeur and significance of this very special occasion.

The wedding invitations specified a dress code: dress uniform, morning coat or lounge suit for gentlemen, and day dress and hat for ladies. Among the non-royal guests were George and Amal Clooney, Idris Elba, James Corden, Sir Elton John, along with Serena Williams and Oprah Winfrey, who would later record an exclusive – and shocking – television interview with Harry and Meghan. Some years earlier, Diana had apparently considered giving Ms Winfrey the broadcasting opportunity of the decade but decided against it when she discovered the format of the show was not what she thought it might be.

The cost of the wedding, which was paid for by the groom's father, may have raised a few eyebrows but it was an event enjoyed throughout the globe, with the television audience estimated to be some 1.9 billion.

Harry already had the use of Nottingham Cottage at Kensington Palace and this became the first residence of the newly-weds, who later moved into Frogmore Cottage in the grounds of Windsor Castle. Frogmore Cottage is a cottage in name

RIGHT: The Duke and Duchess of Sussex chat to children outside Westminster Abbey following the annual Commonwealth Service on 9 March 2020, which the couple attended with The Queen and other senior royals. It was Harry and Meghan's last public appearance as working members of the Royal Family.

only; by the time Harry and Meghan moved in in April 2019, an estimated £2.4 million had been spent on renovations to the property that now has nine bedrooms, a swimming pool and tennis court.

In January 2020, the Duke and Duchess of Sussex announced their plans to step down as senior royals and move to the United States. Two months later they made their last public appearance as working members of the Royal Family. After moving to America, Harry is said to have paid back the money spent on renovating Frogmore Cottage but also renewed the lease so he and Meghan have a base if they are in the United Kingdom.

On 6 May 2019, the year before the move that stunned the country and the Royal Family, Harry and Meghan's first child – sixth in line to the British throne – was born. Again the couple went against royal tradition, announcing the birth via Instagram, rather than using the customary Buckingham Palace route for royal births. They decided to name their son plain Archie Harrison Mountbatten-Windsor, though his birthright entitles him to the courtesy title Earl of Dumbarton, one of his father's subsidiary titles

Harry and Meghan's second child was born in the USA on 4 June 2021, with dual nationality. She is named Lilibet Diana Mountbatten-Windsor: Lilibet the childhood family name of her great-grandmother, Queen Elizabeth II; Diana, of course, the name of her paternal grandmother. The child is seventh in line to the throne and entitled, as the daughter of a duke, to be styled Lady Lilibet. However, she is unlikely to use that title in America. From September 2022, as grandchildren of the sovereign, under a protocol established by King George V in 1917, Harry's children are officially permitted to be known as Prince Archie and Princess Lilibet.

Following Harry and Meghan's decision in 2020 to seek financial independence and privacy in America, The Queen stripped the couple of their right to use the style His/Her Royal Highness. Harry was later deprived of his military titles, including his post as Captain General of the Royal Marines, arguably his most senior and notable position. At his grandmother's State Funeral in 2022, as a non-working royal he was not permitted to wear military uniform.

Diana had been determined to show Harry that although he was never going to be king he still had an important role to play in the Royal Family. It is almost inevitable that she would have been horrified and deeply distressed at the fallout of his move to the USA, and to see her sons at odds with each other.

RIGHT: Prince Harry travelled to England alone for the funeral of his grandfather, the Duke of Edinburgh, which took place on 17 April 2021. Here he walks behind Prince William and their cousin, Peter Phillips, as they arrive at St George's Chapel for the service.

In another television interview Prince Harry gave in April 2022, he referred to his thoughts on Diana, claiming she was watching over him: 'She's done her bit with my brother and now she's very much helping me. She's got him set up and now she's helping me set up.' He also added, 'I feel her presence in almost everything I do.'

LEFT: Diana arriving for a function at the Serpentine Gallery in Kensington Gardens on 29 June 1994. Her daring little black dress, by Christina Stambolian, caused a sensation.

OPPOSITE: A pensive Diana visiting a mosque in Cairo in May 1992; she wore an elegant green and white dress by Catherine Walker and covered her head with a chiffon scarf, in keeping with Muslim tradition. Her solo trip to Egypt was one of the last she would take as the wife of the Prince of Wales before they separated that December.

A Modern Princess: Diana's New Life

With the collapse of her marriage in 1992 – separation, followed by divorce in 1996 – Diana set out to find a new life for herself as a single parent. Though it was noticed that in the days following their separation Diana continued to wear both her engagement and wedding rings, she wanted to create an independent role outside the Royal Family – but, as the mother of an heir to the throne, she was never able to shed her responsibilities completely, or her image as 'Princess Di'.

It appeared, outwardly at least, that the divorce was accepted with good grace and youthful indifference by William and Harry; in their circle, divorce was not uncommon among their contemporaries, and there was no social stigma attached, though, in comments they have made since, it appears all was not as easy as it may have seemed. Meanwhile, the financial settlement by the Prince of Wales attracted huge speculation by the media. Finally, experts predicted, without any confirmation, that Prince Charles gave his ex-wife around £15 million.

On the romantic side, Diana formed a number of relationships, some of which were terminated quickly; she realised that unqualified love and loyalty would come only from her sons. Among the names mentioned frequently as possible lovers –

LEFT: An arm around
her son: Diana aboard
Mohamad al-Fayed's boat
in St Tropez, July 1997.

RIGHT: Diana in 1995:
she was a regular visitor
to the Chelsea Harbour
Club where she worked
out in the gym to stay fit
and toned.

or maybe just friends – was a former royal protection officer and an international England rugby player, who consistently denied that they had had an affair. In between came James Gilbey, a member of the famous gin family whose name he bore – but it was stressed that he and Diana were just very good friends. The most publicised affair was that with James Hewitt, a former Household Cavalry officer with whom Diana was smitten for a time. Then came Oliver Hoare, an art dealer and friend of Prince Charles, who stayed as a guest at Windsor Castle. Hasnat Khan, a distinguished heart and lung surgeon, was close to Diana from 1995, almost until the day she died in 1997, and he attended her funeral. But it was Dodi Fayed – a successful film producer whose movies included the Oscar-winning *Chariots of Fire* – who was with Diana and died with her in the car crash. Whether he was simply a friend, a wealthy companion or more will never be known. Certainly, Dodi and his father, billionaire Mohamad al-Fayed, wooed Diana for months, even inviting William and Harry on to the family yacht *Jonikal*. Diana made sure her two sons wrote personal letters of thanks to their host.

Left to herself in the days immediately following the divorce, Diana worked hard at keeping physically fit by visiting a gym most days, and she sought the company of people whom she believed would not try to exploit her. Once the publicity of the marriage break-up had died down, Diana began working towards her goal, which was to be taken seriously in her own right. She had discussions with political leaders, including President Nelson Mandela of South Africa, and finally she achieved her aim, taking a role on the international stage as an unofficial but highly influential ambassador. Her crusade for the worldwide banning of landmines touched public conscience in a way that nothing else had done. She had picked exactly the right subject at precisely the right moment.

RIGHT: Diana's crusade to ban landmines led to her meeting landmine victims at an orthopaedic centre in Luanda, Angola, in January 1997.

A Queen of Hearts: The Humanitarian

At one time Diana, Princess of Wales was involved with over 100 charities, which she liked to call her 'Family of Organisations'. At the height of her working life, her patronages included such disparate bodies as Barnardos, Birthright, the British Deaf Association (for whom she learned sign language), the Leprosy Mission, the Malcolm Sargent Cancer Fund for Children, The Princess of Wales Children's Health Camp in Rotorua (New Zealand), Turning Point, Help the Aged, Centrepoint, the National AIDS Trust and Great Ormond Street Hospital. When she accepted an invitation to become patron of a charity, she became a tireless worker and a fearless fighter on its behalf, rarely refusing an invitation to go anywhere on behalf of one of her causes. She may have still looked like the princess she undoubtedly was, but she worked hard in whatever way was necessary to help those in need.

Turning Point was perhaps one of the most unlikely groups for a member of the Royal Family to support. It is the largest national voluntary organisation providing help for people with drug- and alcohol-related problems, and for those recovering from mental illness. When Diana was asked to join them she agreed without

hesitation, on the condition that she was not to be merely a royal figurehead but an active participant in their work. She raised the profile of Turning Point dramatically, and as their Chief Executive explained, 'We have an unpopular client group and without the princess's personal involvement we would never have attracted the public's sympathy to such an extent.' Diana also chose to become actively involved with Centrepoint, a charity which concentrates on providing accommodation for homeless young people who are considered to be at risk. Her philosophy was, 'Nothing gives me greater pleasure than to try to help the most vulnerable people in society.'

In 1993 Diana announced her retirement from public life and relinquished her position with nearly all her charities. She retained a handful, which she continued to support and work for until the day she died, among them the National AIDS Trust. One of the most courageous and important of Diana's public appearances had come in 1987, when was invited to open the first specialist AIDS ward in Britain. AIDS was, at that time, the almost unmentionable disease, with few people prepared to be associated with its care and treatment. Princess Diana sent shockwaves throughout the world when she shook hands with patients suffering from AIDS – and did so without wearing gloves. By that single action she demonstrated that people had no need to fear that the disease might be transmitted simply by touch. From that moment her commitment to the cause was total; she helped raise millions of pounds and, more importantly, increased the public's awareness and understanding at a time when fear and prejudice were commonplace.

The compassionate Diana visited a leprosy hospital in Jakarta, Indonesia in 1989, another in Nigeria the following year and others were to follow; comforting those suffering from this most disfiguring of diseases, she never once flinched or drew away from close contact. She said, 'I am trying to show in a simple action that they are not reviled, nor we repulsed.'

One cannot overestimate the impact that Diana made on the causes she espoused. As a fundraiser she was unequalled; her presence at a function ensured that all the tickets would be sold in hours. Her concern for the dispossessed and the underprivileged knew no boundaries. Together with her friends Imran and Jemima Khan, in the 1990s she visited Pakistan to support their efforts in famine relief. She also met Mother Teresa a number of times: the two of them were together for the last time in New York in 1997. But it was when Diana visited Angola and Bosnia, also in 1997, that people realised how sound her instinct was. She had begun her campaign for the banning of landmines without any official backing; when she was accused of interfering in political issues, Diana replied, 'I am not a politician. I am a humanitarian.' But soon governments around the globe were responding to her call.

In Bosnia she met and comforted mutilated victims and bereaved parents, widows and orphans, with a sensitive professionalism that showed clearly how much she understood the anguish all around her. It was to be her last crusade.

RIGHT: On 10 August 1997, Diana was in Bosnia to raise awareness about landmines. Here she comforts a mother whose soldier son had been killed by a landmine.

England's Rose: The World Mourns

Diana, Princess of Wales died in a car crash in Paris, along with Dodi Fayed, on 31 August 1997. Few events in Britain's history have produced the sense of national – or indeed international – dismay and bewilderment that followed. And even though Diana and Prince Charles were divorced, to his credit he, together with Diana's two sisters, took the responsibility of flying to Paris and bringing her body back to Britain.

Her Majesty The Queen gave permission for the use of an aircraft of No. 32 (The Royal) Squadron, which in 1995 was formed from what was previously known as The Queen's Flight. Diana's coffin, draped with the Royal Standard with an ermine border (which is the way that members of the Royal Family, other than the sovereign, have their coffins marked differently) was brought to RAF Northolt in London via Vélizy-Villacoublay Air Base in Paris. Diana was taken to the Chapel Royal at St James's Palace before being transferred to Kensington Palace the night before the funeral. Although Diana's death was sudden and unexpected, the Royal Household moved with rapid urgency and their usual attention to detail to make the arrangements.

Every member of the Royal Family has a code name for their funeral plans which are updated regularly. Diana's was based on that which had been in operation for the Queen Mother for over 20 years. That code name was Operation Tay Bridge and when the moment arrived everything worked perfectly, with very few changes necessary.

People travelled to London from all parts of the country to pay tribute to the Princess of Wales. Thousands of bouquets of flowers were placed at the gates of Buckingham Palace and Kensington Palace, and people queued for up to 12 hours to sign the books of condolence at St James's Palace. The day before the funeral, The Queen appeared on television and spoke movingly of her former daughter-in-law: 'She was an exceptional and gifted human being. In good times and bad, she never lost her capacity to smile and laugh, nor to inspire others with her warmth and kindness.'

The royal ceremonial funeral, described by Buckingham Palace as 'a unique service for a unique person', was a perfect combination of traditional ritual and informality. The coffin containing Diana's body was carried on a First World War gun-carriage drawn by six black horses accompanied by nine members of the King's Troop Royal Horse Artillery, and flanked by a bearer party of Welsh Guardsmen. Thousands, many of whom had camped out overnight in order to get a good position, watched silently, and many threw flowers into the path of the procession. As the cortège passed through Wellington Arch and down Constitution Hill, The Queen and three generations of the Royal Family emerged from Buckingham Palace and bowed their heads. Prince Charles, Prince Philip, Prince William and Prince Harry, together with Diana's brother, Earl Spencer, walked behind the coffin to Westminster Abbey. In adulthood, William admitted that it had been one of the hardest things he had ever had to do, and Harry commented that he did not believe any child should be asked to do what they had done, though later reflected he was glad to have been part of it.

They were followed by a throng of representatives from many of the princess's charities. The service was moving and dignified. Diana's favourite hymns were sung and poems were read by her sisters. Diana's brother gave a penetrating and passionate eulogy which was applauded by those inside the abbey and by the thousands waiting outside. The inclusion of the song 'Goodbye England's Rose' (a reworking of 'Candle in the Wind') as a tribute by pop star Elton John – a good friend of the princess – came as something of a surprise to some of the more traditional members of the 2,000-strong congregation.

The congregation included statesmen, politicians, show-business celebrities, personal friends and representatives from her charities. The television audience in Britain alone was estimated at over 32 million, while worldwide it was said that more than two billion people watched the event, making it at the time one of the biggest ever televised. For many, one of the most poignant elements of the ceremony was her sons' wreath on the coffin: a small ring of white roses bearing the word 'Mummy'. As the choir sang a haunting anthem, the coffin was carried away. At the door the procession stopped and absolute silence descended – a silence that was respected by millions throughout the world. Diana's body was later laid to rest at Althorp, on a peaceful and secluded island in the middle of a lake.

RIGHT: Surrounded by floral tributes to her royal friend: America's First Lady Hillary Clinton in London for Diana's funeral. Representing President Bill Clinton and the American people, Mrs Clinton said, 'We can honour Diana's memory by continuing her work … by reaching out to those who are stranded on the outskirts of hope and opportunity ….'

LEFT: On what would have been their mother's 46th birthday, William and Harry hosted a Concert for Diana at Wembley Stadium. The event raised funds for Diana's charities and those supported by the princes.

OPPOSITE: Marking Diana's 60th birthday on 1 July 2021, Prince William and Prince Harry met with sculptor Ian Rank-Broadley for the unveiling of a statue of their mother in the Sunken Garden at Kensington Palace.

Diana: Remembered by Her Sons

Diana will never be forgotten. Still in her prime when she died at just 36 years old, she was beautiful, elegant, single and sought after by some of the world's most eligible men. It is difficult now, if not impossible, to imagine her as she would be had she lived, a mature grandmother in her sixties. Would she have remained living in Kensington Palace? Or would she have accepted one of the many offers to go and live abroad? She could have chosen to go almost anywhere, but she never gave the slightest indication that she wanted to leave the country of her birth. If she had, America would most likely have been her first choice; over a quarter of a century after her death, her name still attracts much attention in the United States. One thing that is certain is that her two sons, William and Harry, are determined that their mother will always be remembered.

When William became engaged to Catherine he gave her a beautiful sapphire ring. It was of particular emotional impact as it was the ring that his mother, Diana, was presented with on her engagement to Prince Charles. William said, 'It was my way of making sure that my mother didn't miss out on today.' Similarly, Meghan's engagement ring from Harry had Diana connections. The yellow gold circle was

surrounded by '… little diamonds from my mother's jewellery collection, to make sure she's with us on this crazy journey together.'

William and Harry are also carrying on their mother's legacy by continuing her charitable work. William is royal patron of Tusk, a trust which helps protect wildlife across Africa. Diana was patron of a wildlife orphanage in Zimbabwe, which cared for injured and abandoned wild animals. Among his charitable works, in 2013 Harry became patron of The Halo Trust which is dedicated to ridding the world of landmines following conflicts – a continuation of Diana's work following her 1997 visit to Angola.

There are other, highly visible, ways in which Diana is remembered. In the southwest corner of London's Hyde Park is the Diana, Princess of Wales Memorial Fountain. It was officially opened on 6 July 2004 by Queen Elizabeth II, who was accompanied by her husband, the Duke of Edinburgh. Also present were Diana's former husband, Prince Charles, along with her brother, Charles, 9th Earl Spencer, and her two sisters, Jane and Sarah. Sharing the moment were William and Harry.

The fountain had cost some £3.6 million to construct; it was the work of American landscape artist Kathryn Gustafson, who explained the intention of the design was to allow anyone who wished to come and see the memorial to also be allowed and encouraged to walk in its waters. She said the fountain should be accessible to reflect Diana's 'inclusive' personality'.

LEFT: On a hot day, visitors to Hyde Park love to cool off in the memorial fountain, created in Diana's name.

Although Diana's sons have not been on the closest of terms since Harry's marriage, the brothers came together in 2021 to mark the opening of a joint project they had planned four years earlier. In 2017, the 20th anniversary of Diana's death, they commissioned a statue of their mother to be located in the Sunken Garden at Kensington Palace. The statue, which depicts Diana and a small group of children, is the work of British sculptor Ian Rank-Broadley. The garden in which it stands was redesigned and planted with over 4,000 flowers, including forget-me-nots, Diana's favourite flower. The statue was unveiled on what would have been her 60th birthday, 1 July 2021. Of the memorial, William and Harry said, 'Our mother touched so many lives. We hope the statue will help all those who visit Kensington Palace to reflect on her life and legacy.'

The bronze artwork is surrounded by a fence, but there are no restrictions on photography and entrance to the area is free; an admission ticket to Kensington Palace is not needed.

Whatever the differences may be between Prince William and Prince Harry, they are totally agreed on this single issue: Diana will never be forgotten.

The People's Princess: A Tribute

The tragic loss of Diana, Princess of Wales unleashed a tide of public grief on an unprecedented scale, a virtual tsunami of sadness throughout the world, only eclipsed when Queen Elizaeth II died in 2022. Diana appeared to have everything to live for, in spite of the fact that she had been involved in one of the most public divorces of the century, after which she was stripped of what many believed should have remained her rightful style: Her Royal Highness.

So many people had been able to identify with this member of the Royal Family, as a glamorous leader of fashion, a dedicated mother and champion of the under-privileged. She did more than had ever been done before to focus attention on what were previously often taboo subjects, and the practical and constructive way in which she displayed her compassion was a fine demonstration of modern royalty at work.

Diana had star quality, of that there is no doubt. She became the most pursued woman in media history and often gave the impression of enjoying her celebrity status, even though she claimed not to understand why so many people felt so affectionate towards her. Perhaps it was this very innocence that made her so attractive. Although she sometimes gave the outward appearance of being tough

and said she would 'fight like a tiger' for what she believed in, another of the qualities that emerged was her vulnerability, which is possibly why so many people sprang to her defence. Diana never lacked friends to champion her cause, and there was never a shortage of volunteers anxious to protect and cherish her. Much of her international appeal came about because those who came into contact with her felt a fundamental instinct to look after her, even when she protested that she did not need protecting.

Diana has been described as one of the nation's greatest assets. Her appearance was an important attribute; even when her behaviour was unpredictable, she tended to be forgiven because of her beauty, grace and style. Any lack of understanding of her character by the Royal Family was never intended to hurt her. The Queen, Prince Philip and their children had all grown up being taught to ride, hunt and fish almost before they could walk, so they knew what was expected of them. Diana never enjoyed the field sports so beloved by the royals, a potential cause of a separation between them. Diana preferred the city to the country and the idea of spending hours standing around getting cold and wet in muddy fields did not appeal to her; she much preferred fashionable Knightsbridge.

Would it be Diana or Camilla who would have made the best and most suitable queen? It is a question that has been cause for speculation over the years and one that is impossible to answer. They were two very different women. Camilla has proved to